CRYPTOCURRENCY

Cryptocurrency Investing and Cryptocurrency Mining

By Sam Sutton

~~~

CRYPTOCURRENCY INVESTING

The Ultimate Guide About Top Cryptocurrencies for Investing and Perfect Strategies to Make Money

By Sam Sutton

~~~

© Copyright 2018 By Sam Sutton
All Rights Reserved

The transmission, duplication or reproduction of any of the following work including specific information will be considered an illegal act irrespective of if it is done electronically or in print. This extends to creating a secondary or tertiary copy of the work or a recorded copy and is only allowed with express written consent from the Publisher. All additional right reserved.

The information in the following pages is broadly considered to be a truthful and accurate account of facts and as such any inattention, use or misuse of the information in question by the reader will render any resulting actions solely under their purview. There are no scenarios in which the publisher or the original author of this work can be in any fashion deemed liable for any hardship or damages that may befall them after undertaking information described herein. This book should not be taken as financial or investment advice, and the author does not take any responsibility for inaccuracies, omissions, or errors which may be found therein.

Additionally, the information in the following pages is intended only for informational purposes and should thus be thought of as universal. As befitting its nature, it is presented without assurance regarding its prolonged validity or interim quality. Trademarks that are mentioned are done without written consent and can in no way be considered an endorsement from the trademark holder.

The contents of this book are intended to convey general information only. You should not treat any information herein as a call to make any particular decision regarding cryptocurrency usage, legal matters, investments, taxes, cryptocurrency mining, exchange usage, wallet usage, etc. It is strongly suggested that you seek advice from your own financial, investment, tax, or legal adviser. This book should not be taken as financial or investment advice, and the author does not take any responsibility for inaccuracies, omissions, or errors. The author of this work is not responsible for any loss, damage, or inconvenience caused as a result of reliance on information as published on, or linked to, this book.

The author of this book has taken careful measures to share vital information about the subject. May its readers acquire the right knowledge, wisdom, inspiration, and succeed.

TABLE OF CONTENTS

Introduction 7

Chapter 1: Myths About Cryptocurrency Market and
Main Rules of the Market 9

Chapter 2: Basic Principles of Cryptocurrency 15

Chapter 3: Mining Cryptocurrency and
How the Mining Process Works 21

Chapter 4: Blockchain Technology 25

Chapter 5: Wallets and How to Securely Store Bitcoin 27

Chapter 6: Top 10 Cryptocurrencies and
Where to Track Them 33

Chapter 7: Most Popular Cryptocurrency Exchanges 37

Chapter 8: Investment strategies 41

Conclusion 47

INTRODUCTION

Congratulations on downloading this book and thank you for doing so.

The following chapters will teach you everything that you need to know about investing in cryptocurrencies. They will provide you with the right knowledge that will allow you to join the cryptocurrency race, turn the odds in your favor, and dominate the cryptocurrency market. This is your chance to rake in serious and continuous profits.

Chapter 1 talks about the myths that surround the cryptocurrency market and reveals the main rules orfacts behind them.

Chapter 2 discusses the basic rules that you need to know when you invest in cryptocurrency.

Chapter 3 talks about mining cryptocurrency and how the mining process works.

Chapter 4 explains the blockchain technology, which is the backbone technology of bitcoin and other cryptocurrencies.

Chapter 5 explains the different kinds of cryptocurrency wallets, as well as how to securely store your bitcoin or any other cryptocurrency.

Chapter 6 talks about the top 10 cryptocurrencies in the market and where you can track them.

Chapter 7 discusses the most popular cryptocurrency exchanges that you can use to buy, sell, or trade cryptocurrencies.

Chapter 8 reveals powerful and effective investment strategies that you can use to turn the odds in your favour and significantly increase your chances of making high and continuous profits.

May this book be your guiding light to success and financial freedom.

There are plenty of books on this subject on the market, thanks again for choosing this one! Every effort was made to ensure it is full of as much useful information as possible. Please enjoy!

CHAPTER 1:
MYTHS ABOUT CRYPTOCURRENCY MARKET AND MAIN RULES OF THE MARKET

There are myths that surround the cryptocurrency market. As an investor, it is important for you to know the truth behind the myths in order for you to have the right view and understanding of the cryptocurrency market. Let us uncover the facts behind these popular myths one by one:

• *Myth #1: Cryptocurrencies are a big bubble that is about to burst.*

For years, many people have viewed bitcoin and other cryptocurrencies as a mere bubble that is about to burst. Because of this fear, which arises from an erroneous perception, they fail to take advantage of the cryptocurrency market, while those who have the will to take risks and believe in cryptocurrencies have been able to earn a high amount of profit. In fact, some of them have even made their way to complete financial freedom simply by investing in cryptocurrencies like bitcoin, Ethereum, and others. Still, even today, there are those who say that cryptocurrencies are just a bubble. Well, it is up to you if you are going to believe those who claim that it is a bubble. However, the fact remains that while other people think that cryptocurrencies are a mere bubble, there are those who take the risks and believe in the power and value that cryptocurrencies offer, and they are able to rake in serious profits. Whether a bubble or not, it is true that investing in cryptocurrencies can be a very lucrative investment.

The main rule of the market dictates that a cryptocurrency will only "burst" if it has no value or loses its value. But there is no "bubble" to talk about it. This is because bitcoin offers real value to the market. It is widely recognized as a cryptocurrency that can be used for trading.

- ### *Myth #2: Unlike the U.S. dollar, cryptocurrencies have no real value.*

Years ago, the value of the U.S. dollar was pegged to the value or price of gold. However, the dollar was soon weaned off of gold. The result was that the dollar did not have anything to back itself except the faith of the people in its value. The same applies when you use cryptocurrencies. It is the faith of the people that a certain cryptocurrency has a value that allows it to continue to have value and importance in the market. Also, it is noteworthy that many cryptocurrencies these days do not just function as mere substitute for money. In fact, they offer something that makes them even more valuable. For example, the altcoin Ethereum promotes the use of smart contracts and distributed applications on its blockchain. Another example is Ripple, which actually helps banks to have quicker transactions at a lower cost. So, as far as value is concerned, it can easily be said that cryptocurrencies, especially those that are in the mainstream, are highly valuable.

- ### *Myth #3: Cryptocurrencies are for criminals.*

Due to the anonymity enjoyed by cryptocurrency users, there are people who think that cryptocurrencies are primarily created and used for illegal activities like money laundering. However, this is not true. Although cryptocurrency users enjoy a high level of anonymity, they still do not have complete anonymity. This is why those who abused the use of cryptocurrencies to commit illegal acts have already been arrested. Also, if you look at the facts, those who buy guns and other weapon often use fiat money (the official currency of a state) and not cryptocurrencies. Fiat money has been used in illegal activities for many years. This happens even today, especially in the black market.

- ***Myth #4: Investing in cryptocurrencies will only make you lose your investment in the long run.***

Just like any other investment, there are risks involved when you invest in any cryptocurrency. Hence, it is true that you might lose your investment, just as you can also easily lose your investment when you put your money in the stock market, especially if you do not know the ins and outs of the market. In any kind of investment, there are those who make a nice profit and there are also those who lose a part of or even their whole investment. Nonetheless, when you invest in cryptocurrencies, you may or may not lose your investment. In fact, there are so many cryptocurrency investors who have earned a very high amount of profit. Remember the classic example: Had you invested even just $400 in bitcoins back in 2009 or 2010, then you would have earned millions in profit by now. There are many real-life success stories of people who have earned millions in profit. In fact, there are many cryptocurrency investors who have earned their way to financial freedom.

- ***Myth #5: Investing in cryptocurrencies is a fast and easy way to make money.***

Now, there are also those who think that investing in cryptocurrency is a quick and easy way that leads to financial freedom. However, the truth is that even though there are people who have earned millions of dollars and attained financial freedom by simply investing in cryptocurrencies, they are not an everyday occurrence. Many professional and successful traders spend hours on a daily basis just studying the highly volatile cryptocurrency market, and they are very careful whenever they enter or leave a position. Most successful cryptocurrency traders are highly meticulous to details and are very careful with their investment decisions. If you are serious about having continuous success and profit in the cryptocurrency market, then it is a basic rule that you should do hours of research and analysis. Keep in mind that you are dealing with a quickly evolving and highly competitive market

• *Myth #6: The blockchain can easily be hacked.*

Here is the truth: Nobody has ever successfully hacked the blockchain. You may read reports of various cryptocurrency wallets being hacked, but those do not refer to the blockchain network itself. The blockchain is a highly secure system and network that is spread over a vast number of computers. Of course, an attack against the blockchain is possible; however, for an attack against the blockchain to be successful, then the attack must possess at least 51% of the hash power of the entire blockchain network. Needless to say, since blockchain is spread over a vast network of computers, obtaining the said 51% is virtually impossible.

Another bit of good news is that cryptocurrency wallets have already upgraded their security features. In fact, these days, you could barely hear any news of any cryptocurrency being hacked, especially if the person observes certain protective measures, such as using a strong password and enabling two-factor authentication, among others. If you still worry about the security of your cryptocurrency wallet, then you can always use a cold wallet to completely protect it from hackers, malware, and viruses.

• *Myth #7: Governments will prohibit the use of cryptocurrencies.*

The general rule is that the use of cryptocurrencies is legal. If you look at the facts, it is easy to see that almost all governments allow the use of cryptocurrencies in their respective jurisdictions. Over time, more and more states become open to the idea of finally using and embracing cryptocurrencies. A good example of this is Russia, which used to outlaw the use of cryptocurrencies in its territory. In 2017, Russia legalized the use of bitcoins and other cryptocurrencies. Although China closed down all of its local cryptocurrency exchanges, it was for the purpose of preparing some regulations on the use of cryptocurrencies, not for the purpose of permanently isolating itself from the cryptocurrency market. Singapore declared that it would not yet impose any regulation on the use of cryptocurrencies. In many countries, like in the U.S., Canada, Europe, India, Philippines, and many others, the use of bitcoins and other cryptocurrencies is legal. In fact, cryptocurrencies are only prohibited in a very few countries, such as in Ecuador, Bolivia, and Kyrgyzstan, and few others.

Some say that the people behind these cryptocurrencies will soon be arrested. It should be noted that cryptocurrencies like bitcoin are decentralized. This means that there is no person, organization, or authority that exercises control over it. The system works on its own. Hence, there is no one that can be arrested or be put on trial.

- *Myth #8: It is hard to understand the cryptocurrency market.*

Of course, if you read the white paper of a cryptocurrency, you will most likely find it hard to understand because of the technical terms that are used. But cryptocurrencies are easy to understand as long as you are willing to learn and engage in research. For example, by the time that you finish reading this book alone, you will already be equipped with the right knowledge of what cryptocurrencies are about, as well as how you can make an investment and earn a nice profit. In fact, investing in stocks is much more technical than understanding and investing in cryptocurrencies. If you can devote several hours and if you are truly willing to learn, then you can rest assured that you will be able to understand the ins and outs of cryptocurrencies in no time.

So, there you have it. These are the popular myths that surround the cryptocurrency market. Now that you know the truth behind the myths, it is time for you to know the basic principles that govern these cryptocurrencies, so that you will have a much better understanding of what cryptocurrencies really are.

CHAPTER 2:
BASIC PRINCIPLES OF CRYPTOCURRENCY

What is a *Cryptocurrency*?

A *cryptocurrency* is a type of digital asset. It has no physical existence. Instead, it is stored and held electronically (online). It is "crypto" because it is secured using *cryptography*, which refers to the practice of converting information into codes in order to ensure secure communication. Cryptography was used during the Second World War when it was extremely important for the army to ensure that their communications and correspondences were protected against enemy spies. It is a "currency" in the sense that it functions as a substitute for money. Hence, you can use it to buy certain products and services from merchants who accept cryptocurrencies, such as Microsoft, Steam, Peach Airlines, Virgin Galactic, Fiverr, and Overstock, among many others. To date, there are over a thousand different cryptocurrencies in the market, and the number keeps on increasing.

Cryptocurrency vs. Fiat money

Although a cryptocurrency like bitcoin may be used as a medium of exchange, it is still not considered as *fiat money*. What is fiat money? Fiat money refers to the official currency of a state, which is regulated by its government. An excellent example of fiat money is the U.S. dollar. This is because a cryptocurrency is decentralized, which means that there is no person or group that exercises authority over it. This makes it free from all forms of manipulation and undue advantage. Since cryptocurrency is not considered fiat money, it is also not considered *legal tender*. Legal tender refers to that which a "debtor may compel a creditor to accept payment." Of course, the exception to this is if payment in cryptocurrency is agreed upon by the parties in their contract.

It is noteworthy that although a cryptocurrency is neither fiat money nor legal tender, it is still widely accepted by numerous businesses and individuals around the world. In fact, over time, the number of cryptocurrency users has been constantly increasing. Indeed, so many people these days are very eager to learn and understand how to use (and invest) in cryptocurrency.

Bitcoin vs. Altcoins

Bitcoin is the number one cryptocurrency in the world. Back in 2008, a paper was published on a cryptography mailing list. The paper was entitled *Bitcoin: A Peer-to-Peer Electronic Cash System* under the name Satoshi Nakamoto. The following year, bitcoin was finally launched in the market. Back then, bitcoin did not have any substantial value. In fact, just like all other cryptocurrencies (altcoins), it was the cryptocurrency community members themselves who decided the value of bitcoin. There was even a transaction where two pizzas delivered by Papa John's were bought for 10,000 bitcoins. You can still see how this transaction took place on the *bitcointalk* forum, and you will also see other comments that obviously reflect that the people did not take bitcoin seriously at that time. Today, bitcoin is the most successful and highly-priced cryptocurrency in the world. As of January 18, 2018, the price of 1 bitcoin is around $11,600 USD.

To date, there are more than 1,000 different cryptocurrencies in the market. Still, bitcoin is recognized as the number one and most successful cryptocurrency in the world. In fact, it has so strongly established itself that it is now considered as the leading standard of all cryptocurrencies to the point that all other cryptocurrencies are merely called as *altcoins*, which is short for *alternative coins*.

However, it is noteworthy that investing in altcoins can also be a highly lucrative investment. For example, in 2017, the altcoin known as OmisgeGO increased by more than 1,200% in price in just several weeks. Also in 2017, the altcoin, Ethereum, which is the second most successful cryptocurrency in the market and is currently the next in rank to bitcoin, increased by over 13,000%.

Anonymity

Cryptocurrency users enjoy a high level of anonymity. In a transaction, the name and other personal details of the parties involved remain private. Instead of revealing personal details, only the cryptocurrency wallet address, amount involved, and the time stamp are usually the things that are shown to the public. Hence, if privacy is a concern, you will definitely find using cryptocurrencies very helpful. In fact, some cryptocurrencies like Zcash and Dash will allow you to almost completely hide or make private your transaction.

How a cryptocurrency transaction works

A cryptocurrency transaction may not always work the same way, depending on how its blockchain system is structured. However, the usual cryptocurrency transaction, such as when you use bitcoins, has three main parts:

✓ **Input**

Before anyone can send any cryptocurrency to another, it is only logical that he must first have enough cryptocurrency to send in his cryptocurrency wallet. This means that he must first receive cryptocurrency from another. This is what is referred to as an *input*. Once you have an input, then you can start sending or using cryptocurrency.

✓ **Output**

The output refers to the recipient's cryptocurrency wallet address. Take note that a single cryptocurrency wallet can generate multiple different addresses. The *output* refers to the wallet address of the recipient that will receive the cryptocurrency that you will send.

✓ **Amount**

The *amount*, of course, refers to the amount involved in a transaction; therefore, if you are going to send 1 bitcoin, then the *amount* involved in the transaction is 1 bitcoin.

Additional notes

When you are the one who is sending cryptocurrency to another, be sure that you get the right cryptocurrency wallet address. Every cryptocurrency wallet address is unique from the others. It looks like a string of randomly-generated letters and numbers. Once a transaction is confirmed, there is no way that you can cancel or change it, so make sure that you send the cryptocurrency to the correct wallet address. Sending cryptocurrency is fast and easy, especially if you are using a hot wallet. If you are using a cold wallet, then this might take a longer time. The different types of cryptocurrency wallets will be discussed later in the book.If you are the recipient (receiver), then all that you need to do is to give your cryptocurrency wallet address to the sender and wait for him to send you cryptocurrency.

Why Invest in Cryptocurrency?

It is true that although a cryptocurrency functions as a substitute for money, the majority of cryptocurrency holders do not use it as a medium of exchange. Instead, they buy and sell cryptocurrency as a form of investment. Is it lucrative enough? Well, just remember the classic example: Had you invested even just $400 in bitcoin back in 2009 or early 2010, then you would have earned multimillion dollars in profit by now. Needless to say, bitcoin is not the only cryptocurrency in the market that is worth investing in. There are also many altcoins in the market whose price surge as high as 2,000% (and even way higher) in just a short span of time. So, is it profitable to invest in cryptocurrency? The answer is a resounding *yes*. However, just like any other investment, there are also risks involved when you invest in cryptocurrency, and this includes the risk of losing your whole investment. This is the reason why professional and successful cryptocurrency investors use strategies. When you use effective and powerful strategies, you can significantly increase your chances of making the right investment decision. Do not worry; these strategies are also revealed in this book. So, just keep on reading and learning, and you will soon gain a strong foundation to be able to dominate the cryptocurrency market and use it to your advantage. One thing is certain: If you are serious about making continuous profit by investing in a cryptocurrency or different types of cryptocurrencies, then you should be willing to spend hours in research. Just like anything that is worth pursuing, success in the cryptocurrency market requires time, efforts, practice, and hard work.

High volatility

The cryptocurrency market is known for having high volatility. What is *high volatility*? It means that the price of a cryptocurrency usually rises and falls rapidly and significantly. This allows its price to fluctuate and increase by more than 50% (or higher) in 24 hours. Of course, the opposite is also true, which means that its price can drop quickly. This is why you need to study and analyze the market, so that you will be more able to predict the price direction that a particular cryptocurrency will take. Indeed, the cryptocurrency market has a very high volatility. In fact, this is the reason why some investors are afraid to invest in ay cryptocurrency since a market with a high volatility also involves a high risk. However, if you come to think about it, it is not really something that you should be discouraged of. You have to realize that it is exactly the high volatile nature of the cryptocurrency market that makes it a very lucrative investment. It is exactly why you could profit by more than 20,000% in a short span of time. Although there are risks involved, as can be expected of any worthy investment, there are strategies that you can use to turn the odds in your favor and significantly increase your chances of making a highly profitable investment.

CHAPTER 3:
MINING CRYPTOCURRENCY AND HOW THE MINING PROCESS WORKS

Let us discuss another interesting topic in the world of cryptocurrency known as *mining*. Mining is another investment option that you have when you deal with cryptocurrencies. So, what is *mining*? Mining refers to the process of verifying and adding transactions or blocks on the blockchain. The blockchain is the central technology of bitcoin and other cryptocurrencies. It is composed of a record of transactions known as *blocks*. There is a constant demand for miners because without the miners, no new record or block can be added to the blockchain. This means that no transaction can be completed. Hence, mining is a very important activity.

How Does It Work?

Before any new record is added to the blockchain, it must first undergo a process of confirmation and verification. This is what mining is all about. The first thing that a miner does is to verify whether or not a certain transaction is valid or not. Next, a miner will bundle the recent transactions into a block. After that, the miner selects the header of the latest block and connects it to the new block as a hash. The next step is the most difficult part, and that is to solve the Proof of Work (PoW). This is where a miner solves a difficult mathematical puzzle. Once the miner is able to find a solution to the puzzle, only then will the block be added to the blockchain. Hence, this is the time when a transaction will be fully completed. Miners are compensated usually in the form of a transaction fee every time they are able to mine a block. This is the usual way that mining works. Of course, depending on how the system of a certain cryptocurrency is structured, the mining procedure may have some differences.

How to Mine Cryptocurrency

There are several ways to mine cryptocurrency. Let us discuss them one by one:

✓ Computer Mining

You can use your computer to mine cryptocurrency. This is also known as CPU mining, since you will be mining using the power of your computer's CPU. This is a good way to experience what it feels like to actually mine cryptocurrency. You simply have to download the software, and then you can use your computer to start mining. There are free mining software options that you can download online. A popular mining software that you can use is the GUIMiner. It should be noted that you cannot expect to earn a decent amount of cryptocurrency if you only mine using your computer alone. The reason is that a computer does not have sufficient mining power to mine blocks quickly. You will most probably end up with more electricity expenses than the total amount of cryptocurrency that you can mine. Hence, only consider computer mining as way to partake of the actual mining experience, but do not expect to earn any profit from it. Also, when you use computer mining, you should be cautious of overheating problems. You should pay attention to this since too much overheating may break your computer. Be sure to give enough time for your computer to cool down.

✓ Hardware Mining

Since a computer alone does not generate enough mining power to earn you a decent amount of cryptocurrency, the better approach is to do hardware mining. Hardware mining makes use of hardware in order to increase your mining hash power. There are various mining hardware options that you can find online. You might want to check Amazon and eBay. Take note that even if you use hardware, you will still have to use your computer. Hence, you should still be careful with overheating issues. Be sure to give your computer and your hardware enough time to cool down. A major drawback of using this mining approach is that good-quality mining hardware can be expensive, and it will take time before you can fully recover your expenses and break even. In choosing your mining hardware, you should pay attention to the mining power and the electricity consumption. Figure out the necessary computation to see how much you will most likely earn. It is not uncommon to find a bit of strong mining hardware that also spends much electric power. And it is worth repeating that you should pay attention to any overheating issues.

✓ **Cloud Mining**

Cloud mining is probably the most popular and recommended method of mining cryptocurrency these days. When you use cloud mining, you will no longer have to worry about purchasing any hardware or any overheating issue. You do not even have to use your computer. In fact, you do not even have to mine cryptocurrency. All that you need to do is to relax and wait for your mining company to send to you your cryptocurrency, which is usually on a weekly basis or as soon as you reach the minimum threshold amount. Okay, this seems too good to be true. So, what is the catch? The catch is that before a cloud mining company begins to mine for you, you must first make an investment (pay the cloud mining company). A typical offer may look like this: Invest 0.5 bitcoins and receive 0.008 bitcoins every week. At first glance, this seems like a really good deal. You just need to do a simple computation, and you will be able to tell when you will recover your investment, and then the profits that you can earn. However, the problem here is that the offer is usually just the *expected* return and does not refer to the actual return that you will receive. Therefore, there is the possibility that you might receive less than the agreed amount. In our given example, it could be less than 0.008 bitcoins every week. Not to mention, there have been reports where investors did not receive any payment or profit from their cloud mining company. Therefore, be careful since there are many scammers out there. It is important that you only work with a trustworthy and reliable mining company. Before you invest or make any form of deposit, be sure to check the latest ratings and reviews given to the cloud mining company.

It is also not uncommon for cloud mining companies to fix an expiration date to the contract. Hence, you should be able to get back your investment and also make a good amount of profit before the contracts expires. Once the contract expires, then the cloud mining company will no longer mine for you. In order to renew the contract, you will have to pay the mining company again. It is noteworthy that some cloud mining companies may allow you to have a lifetime contract with them. Just be sure to check the terms and conditions of the contract. As can be expected, those that offer a lifetime contract will most likely be the ones that will offer a low return. Regardless of the duration of the mining contract, make sure to read and understand all of the provisions in the contract. This is also a good time for you to hire a good lawyer to make sure that the contract is fair and reasonable before you make any investment, especially if you intend to make a big investment.

Although mining cryptocurrency can still be a highly profitable activity, many experts advise that if you want a better way to earn cryptocurrency and without any limitation to the profit that you can earn, then you should learn investing directly on cryptocurrencies instead of mining them. There are different investing strategies that you can use to increase your chances of making a high amount of profit, as revealed in this book.

CHAPTER 4:
BLOCKCHAIN TECHNOLOGY

Blockchain technology, or simply known as *blockchain*, is the backbone technology of bitcoin and other cryptocurrencies. The first decentralized and public blockchain was developed by Satoshi Nakamoto, the man behind the number one cryptocurrency of all, bitcoin. Bitcoin, as well as other cryptocurrencies, uses the blockchain technology. So, what exactly is this blockchain technology? Blockchain is a public, decentralized, and distributed ledger. Hence, it functions as a repository of all transactions. It also has a very high level of security.

A blockchain is composed of records known as blocks. Every new block that is added to the blockchain must first be verified and pass through a series of confirmations. This is to ensure that the record that is being added is legitimate and genuine. Once a record is added to the blockchain, it can no longer be removed, altered, or withdrawn. Every new block that is added is connected to the previous block using what is known as a hash pointer. This makes all the records or blocks on the blockchain to be interconnected with one another. No part of the blockchain can be amended, changed, removed, or in any way be modified, unless there is a concurrence of at least a majority (51%) of the users in the network. Take note that the blockchain is connected to a vast network of computers. As a distributed ledger, any changes or additions made to any of the records will be reflected to all other users. Hence, if a certain record is added, then such record will be distributed to all the other users in the network, and so they will also be informed about it.

The blockchain is public in the sense that all transactions are viewable and verifiable to everyone. Do not worry; as we have already discussed, all of your personal information remains confidential. The blockchain is also known for being decentralized, which means that there is no central authority or organization that exercises control over it. Therefore, you can rest assured that it is free from any and all forms of bias, manipulation, undue control, and advantage.

As we have already discussed, blockchain technology is highly secure. For an attack against the blockchain to be successful, it must possess at least 51% of the total hash rate of the entire network. Since the blockchain is spread over a vast computer network, obtaining the said 51% is virtually impossible.

Today, blockchain is gaining popularity of its own apart from it being associated with the use of cryptocurrencies. This is because blockchain technology can also be applied to things other than cryptocurrencies and financial-related matters. In fact, those who people who may not like cryptocurrencies are very much interested in exploring possible opportunities of using blockchain technology.

CHAPTER 5:
WALLETS AND HOW TO SECURELY STORE BITCOIN

Why do you need a bitcoin wallet? Well, before you can start using and investing in bitcoins, you first need to have a place where you can store bitcoins. The place where you keep or store your bitcoins is what is known as a bitcoin wallet. There are different kinds of bitcoin wallets that you can use. You should understand their differences so that you will know just which wallet type will best suit your needs. Here are the different types of bitcoin wallets:

• *Web Wallet*

A web wallet is also known as an *online wallet*. This is the most commonly used type of bitcoin hot wallet in the world. Good examples of a bitcoin web wallet are Coinbase, GreenAddress, and Exodus. A web wallet is very convenient to use. You simply have to connect to the Internet to manage your wallet account. Although there have been security issues with web wallets in the past, it is noteworthy that many web wallets have already upgraded their security features, which makes the possibility of being hacked extremely difficult, if not impossible. It is also very easy to make a web wallet. You simply have to sign up for an account with a wallet provider. The whole signing up process only takes less than three minutes to complete.

• *Mobile Wallet*

A bitcoin mobile wallet is another type of hot wallet. As the name implies, it is the kind of bitcoin wallet that you can download on your mobile phone. Many web wallets also function as a mobile wallet. Normally, you can download the mobile wallet as an application from the Apple and/or GooglePlay store. These days, it is very easy and convenient to just use your phone to access the Internet. A mobile wallet will allow you to manage your account, send and receive bitcoins, and even buy and sell bitcoins, simply by using your mobile device.

- *Desktop Wallet*

A bitcoin desktop wallet is a type of cold wallet. Hence, it has a greater security than the aforementioned hot wallets. When you use a desktop wallet, you will store your bitcoins in a computer. The computer does not necessarily have to be a desktop computer. A laptop computer will also work just fine. Keep in mind that unlike a hot wallet, a cold wallet is not exposed to the hazards of the Internet. Therefore, when you use a desktop wallet, you should not connect the computer to the Internet anymore in order to keep it secure and protected.

- *Hardware Wallet*

A hardware wallet is another type of bitcoin cold wallet. It is also like a desktop wallet, but instead of keeping your public and private keys in a computer, you store them in some form of hardware, such as a USB. There are now specialized wallets being sold in the market precisely for this purpose. One of the most popular and highly recommended hardware wallets is the *Ledger Nano*. Just like when using a desktop wallet, you should avoid connecting your hardware wallet to a computer that is connected to the Internet or a computer that is affected by a virus or any kind of malware. This is an important preventive measure to keep your hardware wallet safe and secure. Again, when it comes to using a cold wallet, the main priority is the security of your wallet account.

- *Paper Wallet*

A paper wallet is where you store and print your public and private keys on paper. This is a very popular kind of cold wallet. It is suggested that you print several copies just in case you lose a copy. Needless to say, you should store them in a safe place. It is also common for a paper wallet to have a QR code that you will need to scan before you can access your account and transfer funds. Simply put, you need to be in possession of the paper wallet in order to gain full access to your bitcoin wallet account.

Which Wallet Type Should You Use?

When deciding which type of bitcoin wallet to use, you have to consider how you intend to use bitcoins. If you intend to make regular transactions, then you should use a hot wallet. Most hot wallets are available on the web as well as on mobile; hence, as far as convenience is concerned, you can rest assured that you will not have a problem with it. However, if you just want to make a long-term investment in bitcoin and if you are concerned about the security of your wallet, then you can use a cold wallet. Of course, you are not limited to using just a single wallet. Hence, if you want, you can use both kinds of bitcoin wallets, depending on your needs and how you intend to use bitcoins. You can also use multiple hot wallets at the same time. As the saying goes, "Do not put all your eggs in one basket." The same advice applies when it comes to storing your bitcoins.

Tips to Securely Store your Bitcoins

Regardless of whether you are using a hot or cold wallet, the security of your bitcoin wallet remains of high importance. Here are the best practices that you should observe in order to keep your bitcoin wallet safe and secure:

- *Use a strong password.*

Be sure to use a strong password. A strong password should combine lower and uppercase letters. You should also use numbers and symbols. Needless to say, it should not be something that other people can guess correctly. Therefore, do not use your birthday or your alias as a password. It is also advised that you use a long password of at least 15 characters long. From time to time, you should also update (change) your password.

- *Request a new bitcoin wallet address.*

Most bitcoin wallets will allow you to request a new bitcoin wallet address at any time and as many times as you want. Do not worry; this is very easy to do and you do not have to pay anything. You can do this with just a few clicks of a mouse and in less than 10 seconds. Take note that a single bitcoin wallet can generate many different wallet addresses. It is the wallet address that is used when sending and receiving bitcoins. It is a good practice to request a new bitcoin wallet address for every new transaction that you make. This is an effective way to minimize the exposure of a certain bitcoin wallet address, which is a good preventive measure that can minimize your risk. Again, make it a habit to request and use a new bitcoin wallet address every time that you make a transaction.

- *Check if the page is secure.*

Before you input any sensitive information, like your account password, on a website, you should first see to it that the page is secure. This is easy to do. Simply look at the URL bar and you should see a green padlock and/or the word "Secure" somewhere on the side of the URL bar. This signifies that the page is secure and that it is safe to key in sensitive information. Keep in mind that you should never enter your password or any other sensitive information if you are not sure if the page is secure.

- *Avoid public Wi-Fi connections.*

These days, it is very easy to connect to public Wi-Fi, especially when you are not at home. Although it is okay to use public Wi-Fi, especially if you are just browsing websites, it is not recommended that you access your bitcoin wallet over a public connection. The reason is because there are hackers out there who take advantage of public Wi-Fi connections and use them to pry into other users connected to the public Wi-Fi. A public Wi-Fi is mostly unsecure by nature, so you should not use it if you are going to input any sensitive information or when accessing/managing your bitcoin wallet.

Some notes when using a cold wallet

When you are using a cold wallet, you should make sure that the cold wallet is of good quality. Keep in mind that although a cold wallet can protect you against hackers and all other related Internet risks, it cannot protect you from the risk of having your wallet stolen or broken. Hence, be sure that it is in a good working condition and keep it in a safe place.

(It is noteworthy that these practices are also as effective when you are storing altcoins.)

CHAPTER 6:
TOP 10 CRYPTOCURRENCIES AND WHERE TO TRACK THEM

To date, there are more than 1,000 cryptocurrencies in the market, but only a handful of them are able to draw enough market attention to establish a real value. Let us look at the top 10 cryptocurrencies in the market:

✓ Bitcoin (BTC)

Of course, the first one on the list should be *bitcoin*. Bitcoin is the leading standard when it comes to cryptocurrencies. Indeed, it is the most successful cryptocurrency in the world. As of January 19, 2018, the price of 1 bitcoin is around $11,572 USD.

✓ Ethereum (ETH)

Ethereum is considered by many as the second most successful cryptocurrency in the world. There are even some people who strongly believe that Ethereum will be able to overtake bitcoin and be the number one cryptocurrency in 2018. However, many experts say that this is far from happening, as bitcoin remains very strong in the market. Ethereum promotes the use of smart contracts and distributed applications on its blockchain. Ethereum is the platform, while its cryptocurrency token is known as *ether*. As of January 19, 2018, the price of 1 ether is around $1,058.

✓ **Ripple (XRP)**

Unlike most cryptocurrencies that seem to antagonize banks as if to take their place, Ripple actually helps banks. Ripple was launched in 2012, and it "enables banks to settle cross-border payments in real time, with end-to-end transparency, and at lower costs." Also, unlike other cryptocurrencies, Ripple is structured in such a way that it does not need mining. As of January 19, 2018, the price of Ripple is around $1.64 USD.

Zcash (ZEC)

Zcash was introduced in the market in 2016. It is based on a decentralized and open-source system. Zcash defines itself as follows: "If Bitcoin is like http for money, Zcash is https." Zcash gives primary importance to privacy. It allows the use of selective transparency. This selective transparency allows its users to enjoy a high level of privacy by hiding the details as to the sender, recipient, and even the amount involved in a transaction. This is referred to as a "shielded transaction." As of January 19, 2018, the price of 1 Zcash is around $501.

✓ **Dash (DASH)**

Dash used to be known in the market as Darkcoin. Dash is structured in such a way that its transactions can be made to be almost untraceable. It was introduced in the market in 2014, and it was able to quickly establish a name for itself. Although its name changed from Darkcoin into Dash, its features remain the same. The term, Dash, is short for Digital Cash. As of January 19, 2018, the price of Dash is around $849.

✓ **Litecoin (LTE)**

Litecoin was released in 2011. Hence, it is not a new cryptocurrency player in the market. It is one of the early competitors of bitcoin. If bitcoin was considered gold, then Litecoin wanted to be the silver version. Its features closely resemble those of bitcoin.

However, Litecoin has a faster block generation than bitcoin, and this means that it can confirm and complete transactions much faster than bitcoin. As Proof of Work (PoW), Litecoin uses what is known as "scrypt." As of January 19, 2018, the price of LTE is around $196.

✓ Monero (XMR)

Monero was made out of the donations coming from the cryptocurrency community. It was introduced in the market in 2014. Its main focus is on decentralization and scalability. It promotes the use of ring signatures. When you use ring signatures, a legitimate transaction gets mixed up with a set of false transactions. This is an effective way to "hide" or make your transactions private since people will not be able to identify the legitimate transactions from those that are false, especially that the false transactions will also appear and look as if they were valid. AS of January 19, 2018, the price of XMR is around $337.

✓ Lisk (LSK)

Lisk is quite a new cryptocurrency. It was introduced in the market in 2016. It functions like Ethereum in the sense that it allows the use of applications on its blockchain. When you use Lisk, you can create your blockchain on top of the Lisk blockchain. As of January 19, 2018, the price of Lisk is around $23.

OmiseGO (OMG)

OmiseGO was launched in 2017, which makes it a fairly new cryptocurrency. It aims to provide a simplified and more effective financial service. Its slogan is "Unbank the Banked." It is one of the altcoins in the market that is based on Ethereum blockchain. In 2017, the price of OMG increased by more than 1,200% in just a few weeks. As of January 19, 2018, the price of OMG is around $17 USD.

✓ NEO (NEO)

NEO is known as China's largest cryptocurrency. It was launched in 2014 under the name *Antshares*, but it was renamed later on to NEO by its developers. NEO is also the name by which this cryptocurrency is commonly known. People also call it as China's Ethereum. It functions just like Ethereum. NEO is China's first and number one coin. NEO has also seen a significant increase in price in recent months. As of January 19, 2018, the price of NEO is around $145.

Additional Notes:

The prices of these cryptocurrencies fluctuate continuously. You can easily track their prices by visiting the following sites:

https://coinmarketcap.com/
https://www.coingecko.com/en

CHAPTER 7:
MOST POPULAR CRYPTOCURRENCY EXCHANGES

If you do a search online, you will find many different cryptocurrency exchanges. As an investor, it is important that you work with a trustworthy and reliable exchange platform. Let us look at the most popular cryptocurrency exchanges:

✓ **Coinbase**

Coinbase has millions of investors and customers in the world. It is probably the most popular exchange platform in the world. Coinbase makes it very easy to buy and sell selected cryptocurrencies. Coinbase currently offers only three cryptocurrencies: Bitcoin, Ether, and Litecoin. Coinbase has an excellent reputation and is trusted by many professional investors.

✓ **Kraken**

Kraken started in 2011. It offers many types of cryptocurrencies, including Ripple, Monero, ICONOMI, and other altcoins. It does not just allow you to buy and sell cryptocurrencies, but you can also trade bitcoins with fiat money, such as the U.S. dollar, Japanese Yen, and others.

✓ **Cex.io**

Cex.io also provides different cryptocurrencies to choose from. Just like Kraken, it also allows you to trade cryptocurrencies with fiat money. It also offers a cold storage. It also provides a simple way to buy bitcoins at a price that is close to the actual market rate. This is excellent for traders and investors who are just starting out.

✓ Poloniex

Poloniex offers many cryptocurrency choices. It was launched in 2014, and is now one of the most popular cryptocurrency exchanges. Its trading environment looks professional and secure with more than 100 cryptocurrency pairs to choose from. It has a high trading volume. It is also fast and easy to create an account with Poloniex. You would not have a hard time with it even if you are a complete beginner. It also imposes a low fee for trading.

✓ Shapeshift

Shiftshift is one of those rare platforms where you do not even have to sign up for an account. You can trade directly using a direct and straightforward approach. It does not provide any policy for fiat money, but only offers the exchange between and among different cryptocurrencies. This is simplest and fastest way to convert one cryptocurrency into another.

✓ Bitstamp

Bitstamp is not a new platform. In fact, it has been in the market since 2011, and it is trusted by many cryptocurrency investors. It provides its users with high security features, such as two-factor authentication and multi-signature technology. Its customer support is also available round the clock. Indeed, it has earned a good reputation in the cryptocurrency community.

✓ Binance

Binance is another famous cryptocurrency exchange platform. It also has an excellent mobile application. Although it may not offer a professionally designed platform, you can be sure that trading with Binance makes the process really simple and easy. There are also various cryptocurrencies to choose from. The site is easy to use, and it is also recommended by many serious cryptocurrency investors.

✓ Bitfinex

This is considered as one of the largest cryptocurrency exchange in the market. Although it is trusted and used by many investors, Bitfinex already got hacked which resulted to the loss of around $72,000,000 worth of bitcoins. It has also faced several technical issues. Still, many cryptocurrency investors are happy and satisfied with Bitfinex.

CHAPTER 8:
INVESTMENT STRATEGIES

If you want to have continuous success in the cryptocurrency market, you need to apply effective and powerful strategies that can turn the odds in your favor and increase your chances of making a profit. Here are notable strategies that you should learn and practice:

• *Fundamental Analysis*

As they say, "Knowledge is power." When you use fundamental analysis, you need to have knowledge of the fundamentals or the basics. The key to using this strategy is to have as much knowledge and understanding of the cryptocurrency market, as well as the cryptocurrency that you intend to invest in. When you do fundamental analysis, you should make it a habit to be updated on the latest news, especially those that are closely related to the cryptocurrency market, such as news about the economy, market competition, market acceptance, technological developments, and related government regulations, among others. You need to gain as much information as possible. It is a basic rule in investing that the more that you understand the market, the more likely that you can come up with a profitable investment decision.

If you are serious about making money by investing in cryptocurrencies, then it is considered a must that you learn and use this strategy. To give you an idea: When Russia legalized the use of bitcoins in its jurisdiction, the price of bitcoin and other cryptocurrencies increased. However, when China declared that it would shut down its local exchanges, the price of bitcoin and many other altcoins dropped significantly. When it was featured on the news that the co-founder of bitcoin sold all his bitcoins and invested in bitcoin cash (an offshoot of bitcoin), the price of bitcoin fell and the price of bitcoin cash increased. As you can see, by simply gaining basic information and doing your analysis, you can have a good idea on how certain cryptocurrencies will respond in the market. Once you can predict how certain cryptocurrencies will most likely move in the market, you can then take appropriate actions to take advantage of the market and make a profit.

This strategy can be applied even if you are using a different strategy. In fact, this is so important that it has also been referred to as the lifeblood of investment. Whether investing in cryptocurrencies, stocks, bonds, or real estate, you will definitely find this strategy very helpful.

- *Technical Analysis*

If you are more of a visual person, then you will probably enjoy doing technical analysis. When you use this approach, you will have to study charts and graphs that show the price movements (past and present trends) of a cryptocurrency. The concept behind technical analysis is that all the many factors that influence a cryptocurrency have their final effect upon the price. Hence, by simply analyzing the price movements of a cryptocurrency, you also get to deal with all the many elements that affect it. In a way, this is like a simplified version of fundamental analysis.

When you use technical analysis, you need to learn how to read and identify patterns. Yes, patterns do exist from time to time. However, take note that they often come and go. Therefore, do not expect to always see a pattern or trend every time that you look at a certain chart or graph. A common mistake is to force yourself to see a pattern even if there is nothing at all to be seen. You need to keep an open mind. However, once you recognize a certain pattern, then you should be ready to take advantage of it.

Just like fundamental analysis, you can combine technical analysis with another strategy. In fact, many cryptocurrency investors combine both fundamental and technical analysis. According to experts, mastery of fundamental and technical analysis can increase your chances of success by more than 75%.

• *Averaging Down*

This is a good way to earn a high amount of profit. However, this is also an aggressive approach so you need to be cautious when you use it. The best way to explain this strategy is by using an example: Let us assume that you want to invest in bitcoin and that the price of bitcoin is $9,000. If the price of bitcoin increases, then you make an easy profit. However, if the price drops, for example, down to $8,700, then you should make a buy order at the said lower amount. Now, if it decreases again, say, down to $8,300, then you should make another buy order, and so on and so forth. Simply put, you just have to keep buying the cryptocurrency concerned while its price keeps on falling. Now, although this may seem like you are investing in a losing asset, the truth here is that you are actually making a profitable investment. The key to profit here is when the price of the cryptocurrency (in this case, bitcoin) involved recovers either back to its original value (its price when you first applied this strategy), or higher. When this happens, all the buy positions that you have made will experience a nice profit.

This strategy is also a good way to take advantage of the volatility of the market, especially when the prices of cryptocurrencies constantly rise and fall. Although this strategy may seem very practical and profitable, it is noteworthy that it is also highly aggressive, so you need to be careful with it.

• *Buy and hold*

This is probably the most basic strategy that you can use. However, it is worth noting that there are people who have earned millions of profit simply by using this strategy. So, how does it work? As the name implies, it involves buying a particular cryptocurrency and then holding on to it. You should hold on to it as you wait for its price to increase. Once its price increases over time, you can then sell it at a profit. How profitable is this strategy? Well, just imagine having invested in bitcoin four years ago using this strategy, then you would have made a very high profit by now. Although this strategy is often used for a long-term investment, you can also use this strategy for a short-term investment.

Before you apply this strategy, it is important for you to first study the cryptocurrency market. You need to identify the cryptocurrency that is most likely going to increase in price. You cannot just use this strategy at random. You also need to make sure that you are investing in a valuable and profitable cryptocurrency.

- *Altcoin Spread Out*

These days, many investors like to invest in altcoins. The reason is that altcoins, especially the new ones, have such a big room for improvement. In fact, it is not uncommon to find altcoins that increase their value by more than 200% in just a short period of time. When you use this strategy, you should divide your total capital into parts. There is no hard and fast rule as to how you should divide your capital, but it is suggested that you divide it into at least four equal parts. This will give you four chances or investments. If you divide it into four, then it means that you will invest in four altcoins. The key is to invest in a valuable altcoin whose price will most likely increase significantly. Pay attention to new and start-up altcoins in the market as they have a big room for growth and improvement. It is normal for start-up altcoins to increase even as high as 1,000% over time. Hence, even if you divide your capital into four and only one of those four investments turns out to be profitable, there is a good chance that you will still end up in positive profit.There are three points to consider when choosing a strong altcoin: value, effective promotion, and market acceptance. Make sure that you invest in an altcoin that has a good value. It should also be effectively promoted by its developers and its followers/supporters. Last but not least, it should attract the attention and interest of the market.

CONCLUSION

Thanks for making it through to the end of this book. We hope it was informative and able to provide you with all of the tools you need to achieve your goals whatever they may be.

The next step is to apply everything that you have learned and start earning continuous profits. It is time for you to put your knowledge into actual practice. *Now* is the perfect time for you to make a difference and change your life for the better.

Finally, if you found this book useful in anyway, a review on Amazon is always appreciated!

CRYPTOCURRENCY MINING

The Ultimate Guide to Understanding Bitcoin, Ethereum, and Litecoin Mining

By Sam Sutton

~~~

© Copyright 2018 By Sam Sutton
All Rights Reserved

The following eBook is reproduced below with the goal of providing information that is as accurate and as reliable as possible. Regardless, purchasing this eBook can be seen as consent to the fact that both the publisher and the author of this book are in no way experts on the topics discussed within, and that any recommendations or suggestions made herein are for entertainment purposes only. Professionals should be consulted as needed before undertaking any of the action endorsed herein.

This declaration is deemed fair and valid by both the American Bar Association and the Committee of Publishers Association and is legally binding throughout the United States.

Furthermore, the transmission, duplication or reproduction of any of the following work, including precise information, will be considered an illegal act, irrespective whether it is done electronically or in print. The legality extends to creating a secondary or tertiary copy of the work or a recorded copy and is only allowed with express written consent of the Publisher. All additional rights are reserved.

The information in the following pages is broadly considered to be a truthful and accurate account of facts, and as such any inattention, use or misuse of the information in question by the reader will render any resulting actions solely under their purview. There are no scenarios in which the publisher or the original author of this work can be in any fashion deemed liable for any hardship or damages that may befall them after undertaking information described herein.

Additionally, the information found on the following pages is intended for informational purposes only and should thus be considered, universal. As befitting its nature, the information presented is without assurance regarding its continued validity or interim quality. Trademarks that mentioned are done without written consent and can in no way be considered an endorsement from the trademark holder.

TABLE OF CONTENTS

Introduction 53

Bitcoin, Ethereum and Beyond:
What is Cryptocurrency 55

What is Cryptocurrency Mining? 61

What Can You Mine? 65

Getting Your
Hardware and
Building Your Rig 73

Dump for Dollars, or Keep the Cryptocurrency 85

Future of Cryptocurrency 91

Conclusion 95

INTRODUCTION

Congratulations on downloading your personal copy of *Cryptocurrency Mining*. Thank you for doing so.

Welcome to the ultimate cryptocurrency mining guide. If you are a newcomer to the cryptocurrency world, and you're interested in mining, this is perfect for you. You might only be curious about the workings of cryptocurrencies, and this is a perfect primer.

There are a lot of online resources for cryptocurrencies, and many of them tend to be difficult to understand. They are filled to the brim with abbreviations, technical details, and jargon that a beginner may find it hard to decipher. The following chapters were written with beginners in mind. We've done our best to keep the technical jargon to a minimum.

In order to begin mining, reading this book is a good first step, but your research shouldn't stop here. As you start to build you mining rig, or computer, you need to do more research. There are a lot of individual parts that go into mining, so let's dive in.

There are plenty of books on this subject on the market, thanks again for choosing this one! Every effort was made to ensure it is full of as much useful information as possible. Please enjoy!

BITCOIN, ETHEREUM AND BEYOND: WHAT IS CRYPTOCURRENCY

Cryptocurrency is a virtual or digital currency that provides security for its users by using cryptography. This security feature makes it hard to counterfeit. It most endearing feature is it is organic by nature meaning it does not get issued by a central authority. This makes it immune to any manipulation or interference by the government.

Due to cryptocurrency's anonymous nature, it makes them targets for criminal activities like tax evasion and money laundering.

Bitcoin was the first cryptocurrency to catch the public's attention. Bitcoin was created in 2009 by either an individual or group that called themselves Satoshi Nakamoto. By September 2015, over 14.6 million Bitcoins were already in circulation. These Bitcoins have a market value of about $3.4 billion. The success of Bitcoin has resulted in more cryptocurrencies being created like PPCoin, Namecoin, and Litecoin.

Drawbacks and Benefits

It is easy to transfer money between two people with cryptocurrency. Transfers are expedited by using private and public keys to help with security. The transfers are completed with very low fees, and this lets users stay away from the large fees that many financial institutions and banks will charge to do wire transfers.

At the center of Bitcoin is its blockchain that it stores all the transactions on. Every Bitcoin transaction that has ever been done will be on this blockchain. This gives a data structure that could be exposed to threats from hackers. It can be copied on any computer that runs Bitcoin software. Most experts view blockchain as being important to technologies like crowdfunding and online voting. Cryptocurrencies can even help lower processing fees.

Since cryptocurrencies don't have a central repository and are virtual, the currency can disappear if your computer crashes and you don't have a copy of your total currency. The amount a cryptocurrency can be exchanged for a different currency fluctuates a lot because prices change due to demand and supply.

These cryptocurrencies are not immune to hacking. In the short time, Bitcoin has been around, it has had 40 thefts. A few of these thefts were valued at over one million dollars. Many diehard fans think cryptocurrencies is a currency that will hold its value, expedites exchange, is easier to move than hard metals, and government and central banks can't touch it.

Satoshi

Satoshi is the smallest unit of Bitcoin currency. It gets its name from the creator of Bitcoin, Satoshi Nakamoto. Cryptocurrencies only exist in the virtual world, unlike physical currencies like the US dollar or the British pound. A cryptocurrency can be broken up into smaller units like the dollar is broken down into cents and a pound is broken down into pence.

Bitcoin

Bitcoin follows ideas that were written in a white paper by Satoshi Nakamoto. This person or group's identity has never been verified. With the offer of lower transaction fees and being operated by a decentralized authority, it is no wonder why Bitcoin has risen to fame. The market cap for every bitcoin that is in circulation is over $7 billion.

You cannot physically hold bitcoins. The balance is stored in a public ledger along with every Bitcoin transaction in the cloud. Each transaction gets verified by huge amounts of computing power. Governments or banks can't back or issue Bitcoins, and they aren't valued as a commodity. In spite of being a legal tender, Bitcoins has triggered the creation of other currencies known as Altcoins.

Bitcoin's balances are stored in private and public keys that are long strings of letters and numbers that are linked by a mathematical algorithm that encrypts them. The public key is equivalent to a bank account number. This is the address that is published to everyone and where other people can send Bitcoins. Private keys are equivalent to a PIN number and need to be kept a secret. It is only used to authorize Bitcoin transfers.

Satoshi Nakamoto

This entity is the pioneer of cryptocurrency. Satoshi Nakamoto is the biggest enigma in cryptocurrency. It is still not clear if it is a she, he, a person, or a group. What we do know is Satoshi Nakamoto published a paper in 2008 that started the creation of cryptocurrency.

Bitcoin Cash

This is a fork of the Bitcoin Classic that became known in August 2017. This cryptocurrency can increase the block size and allows more transactions to be processed.

Since it was launched, Bitcoin has faced pressure from members of its community about scalability. Its block size which is one megabyte or one million bytes was set in 210. It slows down processing time and limits Bitcoin's potential just when it was getting popular. The limit of block size was put into the code to prevent attacks on the network when its value was very low. The value of Bitcoin has gone up substantially, and its block size has gone up to 600 bytes. This creates a scenario where transaction times would cause delays due to more blocks reaching maximum capacity.

Digital Copy

This is a record of every Bitcoin transaction that has been confirmed and was sent to the peer to peer network. This is a security feature on the Bitcoin platform that was created to help with double spending.

With the rise of cryptocurrencies, it also created a problem called double spending. This happens when a user buys something from two sellers and uses the same Bitcoins. This would be like trying to buy apples from two different vendors but using the same money for each transaction. This just can't happen. To solve this problem, Bitcoin's creators made a process where every transaction gets copied into a ledger and is verified by many different Bitcoin miners that are distributed throughout the network.

Each transaction gets recorded into the blockchain then copied and stored digitally across various networks within the decentralized system. To keep users from spending the same money twice, digital copy makes sure each participant has an encrypted digital copy of everybody's holding. Miners will verify each transaction and add them to the ledgers. By having digital copies in the Bitcoin ledgers, it is impossible for the history of transactions to get compromised. Any user that tries to change a transaction within the ledger for their own gain will not be successful since they can only change their own digital copy. In order for a transaction to be changed in the ledger, the user needs to have access to everybody's copy. This would prove to be very futile.

Bitcoin Unlimited

This is an upgrade to Bitcoin Core that gives larger block sizes. It was created to improve transaction speeds. Several improvements to this software have been proposed. These upgrades focus on increasing how many transactions that the system can do by increasing the size of blocks or speeding up the process.

Blocks are files where the Bitcoin transactions are stored. Every time a block gets completed, it gets put into the blockchain. Blocks are limited in size to one megabyte. Bitcoin Unlimited wants to increase the block size. This means that companies and individuals give the computing power that is needed to keep the records of all the transactions.

Since Bitcoins isn't controlled by a central authority, decisions about upgrades are made through a consensus. Any person or organization that pushes a change forward and the other members didn't agree to it can cause a fork in Bitcoin. This means the network that is running Bitcoin will split. Having a consensus-driven approach could make it hard to tackle issues that Bitcoin faces.

Problems with forking are one reason why Bitcoin Unlimited isn't the new standard. Having larger blocks can result in miners who have larger processing units will be more powerful and profitable, while small miners could get pushed out entirely.

Litecoin

Litecoin was created in 2011. It is a different cryptocurrency that is modeled after Bitcoin. Litecoin's creator is Charlie Lee. He is a graduate of MIT and used to work at Google. Litecoin just like Bitcoin is an open source network that is decentralized. It is different than Bitcoin because it can create blocks faster and uses scrypt as proof of work.

Litecoin was created with the hope of being the left to Bitcoin's right. It has gained popularity since it was created. Litecoin is also a peer to peer network. Litecoin was created to improve on Bitcoin's shortcomings. It has earned support as well as liquidity and trade volume. Litecoin was designed to create more coins faster. Litecoin is considered second to Bitcoin, but Litecoins are easier to get and send.

Altcoin

These are all the different cryptocurrencies that have been created after Bitcoin. They say they are better than Bitcoin, but that is still to be seen. Many alternative coins are targeting the limits that Bitcoin has and creating newer versions. There are many varieties of Altcoins.

Most of the Altcoins are built on Bitcoin's framework and makes the peer-to-peer as well. Some offer more efficient and cheaper ways to send transactions. Even though many features of the Altcoins overlap, they are still very different from each other.

Even with all these competitors, Bitcoin is still the leader in the cryptocurrency pack. Newer versions are being launched. This offer changes in areas such as DNS resolution, proof of stake, privacy, transactions speed, and so much more. Some have gained popularity. Some are not as well knows. Some examples of Altcoins are Novacoin, Zetacoin, Feathercoin, Peercoin, Dogecoin, Litecoin, and others. Litecoin is Bitcoin's closest competitor.

WHAT IS CRYPTOCURRENCY MINING?

As stated earlier, cryptocurrency uses a technique called cryptography to process transactions. This is a process that converts legible information into uncrackable codes that helps keep track of transfers and purchases. For a simple definition, it is just entries in a database that nobody can change without going through specific protocol.

Cryptography used the element of computer science and mathematical theory and was created during World War II to transfer information and data securely. It is now being used to secure money, information, and communications online.

Cryptocurrencies run on blockchains that are shared ledgers and get duplicated many times over a network of computers. An updated document gets made and distributed to anyone who holds cryptocurrency.

Each transaction that gets made and the owner of every cryptocurrency gets recorded onto the blockchain. These blockchains are run by miners that use very powerful computers to verify the transactions. They have to update every time a transaction gets made to ensure the information is authentic. This assures every transaction is processed safely, properly, and securely.

Miners get paid by minted cryptocurrency as payment for their work. These will show up as fees from merchants or vendors.

Cryptocurrency's value goes up and down based on supply and demand. It does not have a fixed value. Seller and buyers agree on a certain value that is fair based on what cryptocurrency is trading for elsewhere.

Transaction fees that are associated with credit cards are eliminated since the transaction is peer to peer. The identities of the seller and buyer are never revealed. Every transaction is public to everybody on the blockchain network.

People can get cryptocurrencies through exchanges online or trade it for normal currencies.

Mining for cryptocurrency has two functions: releasing new currency and adding transactions on the blockchain. Every block that gets added by miners has to contain proof of work.

Miners have to have a computer with a special program that helps them compete with other miners to solve complicated math problems. This takes large amounts of computer resources. Miners attempt to solve a block at regular intervals. They need the transaction's data and use hash functions to solve it.

The hash value is a value of numbers that can identify data. Miners use computers to find hash values less than the target. Whatever miner cracks it first is the one who actually mined the block and will get a reward. The reward for a block sits at 12.5 Bitcoins.

Early on, cryptography enthusiasts were the miners. As Bitcoin gained popularity and its value increased, mining is now a business on its own. Many businesses and people have begun investing in hardware and warehouses.

As businesses jumped on board, they soon realized they couldn't compete. Miners have started opening pools and combining their resources to compete better.

One business, Bank of New York Mellon Corp., has been using a blockchain platform since 2016 to help with US Treasury bond settlements. The privacy of the platform has allowed it to remain out of the grasp of regulatory agencies. When a bank decides to let its clients use it commercially, regulatory agencies might get into the action.

A mining kit contains a fan, cabling, memory, power supply, a processor, and graphics cards. The cost for this is around $2,400 to $3,800 if bought through Amazon. The best hardware for mining is AntMiner S9, AntMiner S7, and Avalon6.

Normal GPUs are not strong enough, so miners are beginning to use ASICs or application specific integrated circuits. To help with this shortcoming, AMD and Nvidia are working on GPUs that might be used just for this purpose.

There are two companies that are dominating the mining hardware, and they are Bitmain and Canaan. Bitmain is located in Beijing. It mines and manufactures hardware.

Mining Pools

Most mining pools are located in China and do about 81 percent of the hash rate. For Nvidia and AMD that dominate the gaming chip market, turning their focus off of their main business might not be a good course of action.

These companies have to create GPUs that were designed exclusively for the sole purpose of mining. These GPUs are a threat to the ASIC chips that are manufactured in China.

Exchanges and governments are contemplating about the regulations of cryptocurrencies. After MtGox, a Tokyo based exchange collapsed in 2014, Japan has introduced laws to protect users. Introducing taxes like a tax on capital gain of Bitcoin sales might slow down the cryptocurrency industry.

WHAT CAN YOU MINE?

Mining for cryptocurrencies and Bitcoin is very popular these days. As more people start mining, it gets harder to mine any type of cryptocurrency successfully.

To maximize your hashing power, you need to mine the currency that offers the most profit. Don't try to mine the difficult algorithms such as Bitcoin, try some easier cryptocurrencies. Once you have successfully mined the currency, convert it into the currency of your choice. You can do with by using an online exchange and thus maximizing profits.

Here are the cryptocurrencies that lead the pack:

- Bitcoin: With today's economy, each transaction we do has to go through the credit card company or a bank. They take out a fee for the transaction, and we have to hope they don't mess up. This is where Bitcoin comes in. At the center of Bitcoin are mathematical problems. Miners have to solve these. When a solution is found, the miner is rewarded with Bitcoins. Bitcoins are mined using powerful graphics cards.

- Ethereum: This platform is designed for people who want to create decentralized applications. In recent months, Ethereum has become very valuable and makes it the best choice for miners who are just beginning. It allows peer-to-peer transfer and a blockchain. This blockchain comes with its own language. This lets people use it for all sorts of decentralized applications. It is secured by cryptography. Ethereum doesn't have an ASIC. This doesn't mean you won't be able to make money. If you have a mining GPU, you can mine about $1,400 per year.

- Litecoin: This is another decentralized cryptocurrency. There is only about 84 million in existence. It offers low fees and quick transaction times. You can sell and buy it from other people and exchanges. You can use it to buy pretty much anything. If you use Antminer, you could mine about $6,000 per year.

- Dash: This is the first cryptocurrency that acts like fiat currency. You keep complete control of your money. You have total privacy, and there is no way to track the transactions. Transactions are processed instantly. There are virtually no fees since you control the money. Dash is one of three currencies that are most profitable. By mining using a specified ASIC, you could mine about $1,000 per year.

- Monero: This cryptocurrency is interchangeable. It prides itself on the privacy it gives to its users. Its value is increasing steadily. Investing in Monero hardware just might be the way to go. If you mine using a specified GPU, you could mine $1,400 per year.

- Zcash: This cryptocurrency is based on Bitcoin's platform but has one main difference. Zcash offers its users the option of encrypting their own transactions. This essentially means that the transaction's amount, the recipient's address, and the sender's address is all hidden from the public. Most think Zcash is the future of keeping transactions anonymous. Normal GPUs are able to mine Zcash like GTX 1080. It can also mine for Decred. Zcash has put a cap on how many coins can be mined. Jump in now as only 21 million will ever be mined.

- ZenCash: This cryptocurrency was made for user privacy. Most call it the privacy coin. All transactions are off the grid. This makes them extremely secure. It allows you to send coins straight to a recipient's address. This would be a great cryptocurrency to learn how to mine.

How It Works

Cryptocurrency creates blocks from all transactions. These get put together and creates a blockchain. Every time a transaction is done, the blockchain gets updated.

Miners use a process where they take the information and use formulas to process it. The result is a string of numbers and letters that is shorter than the actual transaction. This is known as a hash.

Every hash is similar to the hash that gets used first. Because every hash is based on the one in front of it, the next one will confirm the other ones were legitimate.

To mine for blocks, miners use specific GPUs to find answers to questions. When they find the answer, they receive a certain amount of coins as a reward. Miners use header metadata throughout the hash function. Each currency has its own algorithms. Litecoin uses Scrypt. Every time a valid hash gets found, it goes through the network and becomes part of the public ledger.

You are not able to fake your work and cheat. This is why all cryptocurrencies require proof of work. Ethereum is trying to get rid of proof of work and use proof of stake. If the miner can validate their work, they get rewarded with cryptocurrency.

Importance of an Efficient and Powerful GPU

Think about all the information that has been provided and you can understand why a powerful GPU is needed. You will be able to mine coins more successfully if you have a powerful GPU.

Powerful graphics cards use huge amounts of electricity. You need to think about how important the card's efficiency is as well. It might be better to buy several cheaper GPUs that have higher hash/power ratio. It might give you better profits. A good example of this type of GPU is the GTX 1050 Ti.

Mining is getting harder every day, so it is critical to have an efficient GPU. Some will cost you more in electricity bill than they will give you in revenue.

Factors That Harm the Efficiency of a Computer

You are not able to use just any graphics card to mine. Here are some cards to consider:

MHash/s

This is equivalent to how many numbers the card can handle during mining. You will use more hashes if you rate is high. If the hash rate is low, you won't use as many. What exactly does that mean? Higher hash rate means quicker results.

MHash/j

This is the number of hashes that the card can handle per energy joule. As stated earlier, mining uses a huge amount of electricity. Your graphics card will need to mine enough coins in order for you to make a profit after your electricity bill has been paid.

A larger number shows your card is more energy efficient. If the card is energy efficient, then you are saving yourself some money.

MHash/s/$

This is a way to show the performance/price ratio of a card. If it has a high number, you will get more for the money. If a card uses a lot of electricity and has a low hash rate, you won't be creating a lot of revenue, if any.

You need to find a card that has a good balance of performance and price. Mining for cryptocurrencies like Ethereum, Litecoin, and Bitcoin takes a very powerful graphics card. It actually takes several graphics cards. You will also need a motherboard that has the same amount of slots as GPU cards.

Make sure you have the correct power supply. If your computer doesn't have the right amount of power, it isn't going to work correctly.

Is Mining Right For You?

Mining is a great idea. Go out and purchase a mining GPI and watch the money roll in. Right?

Actually, no.

There are large warehouses in different countries that have very low electricity bills. These warehouses are home to thousands of GPUs, and the cost is anywhere from thousands to millions of dollars.

With this huge setup, mining is very profitable, and investors are making huge amounts of money. When an individual is mining on a personal computer at home, they might never see a return on their investment.

You can still benefit from mining. Some do it as a hobby that gives them a little something for their time. Unless you do it on a huge scale, you aren't going to see a whole lot of profits. If you just want to own some cryptocurrency, just purchase some.

Trading Cryptocurrency for USD or Other Cryptocurrencies

You will need to exchange your preferred cryptocurrency for Bitcoins first. Here is how to do it:

1. Create an account in an online exchange like Binance.

2. After the account has been created, now you will need to buy your preferred currency's wallet address. This address gets used with your mining software. The currency you mine gets put into this wallet. From there, you are able to exchange if for Bitcoin and then USD. To do this Hover over the tab that says Funds. A drop-down menu should appear. Now click on deposits/withdrawals. Look for your cryptocurrency and click on deposit. When asked, click agree and move on. You will be sent to a page that will show your personal address. Copy the code and put the software in this address.

3. After you have deposited cryptocurrency into your exchange account, you can decide to change it for Bitcoin. Here is how to do this:

   Go to the exchange's homepage but clicking on the logo. Go to the BTC Markets and look for your cryptocurrency. When you have chosen your currency, you will see it in the search results. Click on it. In the sell box, you can exchange your currency for Bitcoin. If you need to convert all the currency you own into Bitcoin, just choose 100 percent.

4. Now, you will need to transfer your Bitcoins out of the exchange you are using into another one like Gemini or Coinbase. After it has been transferred, you can exchange Bitcoins for USD. Here is how to do it:

   Go back to the deposits/withdrawals page. You can now withdraw your acquired Bitcoins out of your Bitcoin wallet like this:

   Type in your Bitcoin address. Go to either Gemini or Coinbase (whichever one you used). When you have finished the registration, now click on accounts. Click receive under the BTC wallet. You should see a QR code pop up. This is your wallet's address. You will need to copy and paste this into the BTC withdrawal address. Choose your amount and then submit.

5. The final step is to sell you Bitcoin for normal currency. Go to the sell/buy tab and click on sell. Just choose the bank or account you want the money deposited into. Type in the amount of Bitcoin you want to deposit and click sell Bitcoin. That's it.

You have successfully traded your cryptocurrency for Bitcoin and exchanged Bitcoin for USD.

GETTING YOUR HARDWARE AND BUILDING YOUR RIG

For this chapter, we are going to get into the nitty-gritty of building your rig and mining. For the purpose of this chapter, we will look at building and Ethereum rig. This will go through sourcing your equipment as well as putting it together. This could take you up to a week to accomplish. You also have the option of buying a cloud mining contract through Genesis Mining or Hashflare if you are not interested in buying mining equipment.

Sourcing Equipment

You need to get a hold of a lot of components, and the costs can stack up.

1. Motherboard

The brain of your computer, the motherboard is what everything is built into and the base of your rig. The main thing you need to look at for your motherboard is how many GPU slots it has because this will determine how many GPU's or graphics cards it can hold, which is what determines your hashing power. If the motherboard has 3 PCI Express slots, then you will be able to fit 3 x Radeon HD 7950 and have a hash rate of 20 MH/s each, which will give you a complete hashing power of 60 MH/s. The PCI Express slot is the connection spot on your motherboard. They are typically white, but they may be beige. There are other types of slots but for the most part GPU's work on PCI.

2. Graphics card

Now you pick your GPUs. There are some graphics cards out there that will cost you an arm and a leg, but they have horrible hashing power. Then there are others that are more reasonably priced and have more power. You basically need to find a balance between the power you are looking for and how much you are willing to spend. The important thing is that you pick an efficient GPU. You can purchase refurbished GPUs from reputable sites like GPU shack. You have to be careful though; there are a lot of second-hand cards that have problems that you won't discover until you plug them in.

There is one common issue that you can have with your motherboard and graphics card. You may find that they don't all fit together perfectly because of how the PCI Express slots are spaced on the motherboard. Fear not, you can get a riser which works like an extension cable for the slot. There are some graphics cards that are bulky, so be careful when you are choosing your card.

3. Hard drive

The hard drive is needed for you to store your operating system and the mining software on. You can use a standard SSD drive. The size you need will depend on what you want to do when you are mining. If you are interested in downloading the complete blockchain, then you need to consider how large the blockchain will become and the time you need to spend on it. If you plan on mining Ethereum as part of a pool than you won't have to store the blockchain and you will be able to get a smaller SSD drive.

4. RAM

This is one of the most basic components of all computers and works as a scratchpad for writing down calculations and being able to call that information up quickly on your computer. 4GB should be big enough.

5. PSU

You can get power supply units in several different sizes, and this can cause problems for some when they are trying to figure out the size they need. You should add up your GPU's power consumption and all of your other components, and then make sure that that the power supply has a bigger power supply. If you are using two GPUs that use 220 watts and your other components take up another 250 watts, then you can use a 750-watt power supply unit because the complete amount of power you need is only 690 watts. If you plan on building a "mega rig" that contains six GPU's, you may find that it is more cost efficient to use two different power supplies. Two 750 watt PSU at the cost of $100 a piece is better than $300 for a single 1500 watt PSU.

6. A case

This can prove to be fairly difficult choice because it will depend on your GPU's, as well as whether or not you are using risers. You need to make sure you don't have components sitting on top of one another as this is a fire hazard. You can choose to leave your system open air; you can build a case for it yourself to give it a little personalization. You can also choose to buy an off the shelf rig from a few providers. They can take awhile to get to you, but all of the hard work is done.

gpuShack.com is a great website to source your components. They offer group packages, which can make it cheaper for you.

Putting Your Rig Together

Like I said earlier, you need to make sure that your power supply will be able to handle your graphics cards, and then you also have risers that will give you the chance to place extra GPU's in safe place. All of the connections need to be plugged in correctly and that everything is held together.

A word of advice on positioning, GPU's can become hot, especially if they are overclocked, so you need to make sure you get the best bang for your buck. You also need to make sure that your rig is placed in a well-ventilated area so that you don't risk it overheating.

Once your rig is turned on, you will want to make sure that all of the software you need for mining is on your rig.

Software

The first thing you have to do is to install an operating system onto your rig. For people who are more technically minded, you can use Linux Ubuntu, but for most people, Windows is the best choice because it automates installing drivers so that all of the components talk correctly to each other. The best part of Ubuntu, though, is it provides a lot of options and its free.

You can also choose to download EthOs, which is an APP that was specifically designed for Ethereum mining. This is the perfect way a specific mining system for your GPU's and rigs to manage all of them.

After you have downloaded your operating system onto your rig, there are two ways that you are able to start mining:

- Solo mining – this type of mining means that it is you against everybody else. If you create the correct hash, then you will get the block reward. If you have a rig of 60 MH/s and a hashing power of 1.2 GH, you probably won't see much ether. You will also need to download the blockchain.
- Pool mining – this type of mining requires you to team up with other miners to lower the volatility of returns. This could mean that you get five ether every five days, or you get an ether every single day. The best thing about this is that you get a continued stream of ether and you won't need to download the complete blockchain.

Mining Ethereum

You should now have a pretty good understanding of how mining works, so you are probably itching to get started mining yourself. As a little refresher, mining is what holds the 'decentralized app store' together by making sure that there is a consensus for every change to the applications that are running on the network.

Take, for example, the online notebook that is described in "What is Ethereum?" The network was unable to reach a consensus about the notebook's state, as if a note was deleted or added, without computational power to process through the changes.

Miners allow their computers to go crazy to solve cryptographic puzzles in an attempt to get ether, and they need to try a large number of computational problems until somebody can unlock a new asset batch.

A very interesting part of an open blockchain is that, theoretically, anybody can set their computers to only focus on these puzzles as a way for them to win the mining rewards. The problem is that mining on these public blockchains will eventually require even more power over a period of time as more people begin investing in better hardware.

It is now very unlikely for those that are mining with low-powered setups for them to win, but it is still a pretty decent past-time for enthusiast and hobbyists.

As you learned earlier, you need a rig that is solely used for mining. You can choose from GPUs and CPUs, as you know. GPUs will provide you with a better has rated. GPUs are the only option for a person that is interested in mining ether.

Getting your GPU together can be quite complex, so make sure that you get others advice, and don't rely only on this book. Other people may have good advice on the most profitable choices based on hash rate, initial expense, and power consumption.

You can also find mining profitability calculators that will show how much you may be able to earn given your hash rate when set against the electricity cost and setup.

After you have set up your rig, and have taken care of your hardware, you need to get your software ready. Miners will need to install a client that can connect to the network. People who are familiar with a command line can choose to install geth, which will run an ethereum node written in 'Go,' a scripting language.

After you have your software downloaded, your node will be able to talk with other nodes, which will connect it to the Ethereum network. Besides the fact that it can be used to mine ether, it will give you the interface to deploy smart contracts and send transactions with a command line.

Testing

You can also choose to mine 'test' ether on a private network so that you can experiment with the decentralized applications or smart contracts. Mining on a test network won't require fancy hardware on your part. All you will need is a home computer with geth or some other client installed. Minting fake ether isn't going to be all that lucrative.

Install Ethminer

If you are planning on mining real ether, you need to install mining software. After you have downloaded a client and your node has become a part of the network, you will then need to download Ethminer. You will need to find the right download version for your operating system.

After this has been installed, your node will start to play a part in staking your place in the Ethereum network.

Join a Mining Pool

You probably won't be that successful as a sole miner of ether. This is why there are miner pools. Miners 'pool' their computational power together to create a mining pool. This will improve the chances of solving the puzzles and getting a reward for everybody involved in the pool. They will then split their profits proportional to the amount of power the miner contributed.

There are a lot of different factors that are involved in jumping into a mining pool. Every pool probably won't stay around for forever, and the computational power of all of these pools change constantly, so there are a few factors that you need to consider before you decide to join one.

One important thing that you need to remember is that mining pools have different types of payout structures. A mining pool will a signup process on their website so that miners are able to connect with the pool and then start mining.

You have to remember the world of mining is a whirlwind of change. The tools that you learn today could disappear next year, and there are mining pools that may fall away while others are created, so you have to keep an eye out for industry shifts.

Mining Bitcoin

Mining Bitcoin works pretty much the same as mining Ethereum. You will need to have you mining rig set up and ready to go. For the most part, you will probably need to make sure you get an ASIC if you are interested in mining Bitcoin. Otherwise, you probably aren't going to see much in return. You will then need to download the mining software. There are a lot of programs that you can use for Bitcoin, but the most popular choices are BFGminer and CGminer which work as command line programs.

If you want the ease of use that you can get with a GUI, then you may want to download EasyMiner, which works as a click and go Android/Windows/Linux program.

After you have everything ready to start mining, it is best that you join a Bitcoin mining pool. Without using a mining pool, you might be stuck mining Bitcoins for years and never earn a single one. It's a lot easier to share the work and then split the reward a group of miners.

If you want a fully decentralized pool, you can use p2pool. As of right now, the following pools fully validate block using the Bitcoin core 0.9.5 or later:

- Slush Pool
- Eligius
- CK Pool
- BitMinter

No matter what coin you are mining, you will need to make sure that you have a wallet for your coins to be deposited in. Above all else, make sure that you stay up to date on all the current Bitcoin news. This is important for your profits.

Writing Script

If you are planning on using cpuminer, you will need to know how to set up your parameters for mining. It's easier to create a one-line script, called a batch file in Windows, to launch your miner with the right instructions.

For this you will need:

- Worker password
- Worker number or name
- Mining pool username
- Port number for the server

- Stratum URL for the mining pool server
- Full path to the directory where your program is stored

You will then need to open Notepad or your text editor of choice. You should not ever use a word processor like MS word. Next, you will need to type in the script. This method assumes that you are trying to mine a currency that uses the scrypt algorithm.

Start "path" minerd.exe – url URL:PORT –a scrypt - - userpass USERNAME.WORKER:PASSWORD

When you type in the above details, you should get the following:

Start "C:|cpu-miner-pooler" minerd.exe –url stratum+tcp://pool.d2.cc:3333 –a scrypt – userpass username.1:x

You will then need to save this file with a ".bat" extension. After you have saved the batch file, double-click it to activate your new miner program. The mining pool is probably going to have a web-based interface. After a few minutes, the website should start to show that you are actively mining.

GPU Miner Setup

For those that you interested in mining with GPUs, which would be anybody that creates a mining rig, you should use the cgminer program. Versions of cgminer past 3.72, do not support scrypt mining, this means that you shouldn't just download the latest version. You will need to find the version that offers everything you need.

This setup is assuming you are using Windows. If you are using OS X or Linus, the command line arguments are going to be the same.

You need to extract the software into a folder that you are able to find easily. You now need to make sure that your graphics drivers are up to date. You then need to press the Windows key with the "R" key. Then type in the "cmd," and then select enter. This will give you a command terminal. You can then use the "cd" command to switch the directory to the one that has the cgminer file.

Type in "cgminer.exe –n." This will give you the list of the recognized devices on your PC. If it can detect your graphics card, then you can go to the next step. If it does not detect your graphics card, then you need to research the steps required for properly setting up your graphics card. Then make sure you have the information for your mining pool. This is the same information that you needed for the CPU setup.

Now you need to create a batch file so that you can start your cgminer correctly.

Start "path" cgminer – scrypt –o URL:PORT –u USERNAME. WORKER –p PASSWORD

Now you have your chosen mining software set up, you will start to see statistics scrolling through the command line. If you have cgminer, you are going to get more info than that with cpuminer. With the cgminer, you will see information about the mining hardware, mining pool, and currency. If you are using cpuminer, you are only going to see information about the blocks that your computer has solved, and your hashing speed.

The great thing for people who have a PC with dedicated graphics cards, you can run cgminer and cpuminer together. To this, you will add a "-threads n" argument into the minerd command. In this, the "n" stands for the number of CPU cores that you want to employ.

You need to make sure that you leave a few of these cores free to work your GPUs. If you set minerd to use all of your CPU cores your CPU will be too busy to send data to the GPU. If you have a quad core CPU, then you should set the argument to "2" or "3."

When you mine with CPU and GPU, you will be able to see how much better GPUs are when it comes to mining. Look at the hash rates in your terminal window for your programs, and you will likely see at least five times the difference.

DUMP FOR DOLLARS, OR KEEP THE CRYPTOCURRENCY

One of the biggest questions people will ask is which cryptocurrency they should buy. Another commonality for the beginner is that they don't spend most of their day listing to the options of cryptocurrency experts and personalities, doing extensive research, and analyzing the market.

Even if there is some seemingly knowledgeable and trustworthy "expert" that tells you that you need to invest in cryptocurrency A or B, a beginner doesn't have the business experience or technical skills to evaluate if this is or isn't a person that you can trust.

One thing is for certain; beginners aren't interested in getting into a coin that has huge volatility and an unknown future. This means that it only makes sense for them to get into coins that are built on solid tech, a strong team, and solid business plan.

When you have mined or bought cryptocurrencies, there are few things to look at so that you can figure out if you should keep it or sell it for dollars:

- Is there a highly reputable team backing this coin?
- How active are they in improving and maintaining their coin?
- Are they actively communicating with their investors?
- Is the coin blockchain based?
- How many coins are in circulation and what is a total number of coins?
- How much are they worth?
- How many coins were premined and are you able to mine them?

- How many exchanges have these coins?

Now that we have gone through some important steps you should take, let's look at the coins that I would suggest holding onto. This should not be used as investment advice; it's only an opinion.

Steem

This cryptocurrency is used on the social media blogging platform Steemit. They also have a Steem dollar, which means they have two cryptocurrencies. The Steem dollar will only ever be worth a dollar, whereas Steem's value will depend on the market.

I believe most of its value comes from Steemit. Platforms such as Twitter and Facebook aren't incentivized. You have a greater chance having to pay them to use the site, than making money from it. Steemit gives you the chance to make Steem dollars and Steem by posting quality content. You can blog for money on Steemit, but the upvotes you receive for your content is what determines the amount you earn.

You can also power up your Steem by using Steem power. Steem power is what decided the worth of your vote. If you were to have 1,000 Steem power, your upvote would be worth 20 cents. But, if you have 500,000 Steem power, the upvote would worth $100. Basically, you are encouraged to spend money on Steemit.

If you want to withdraw money, you will have to wait three months to power down. This keeps people from being able to move money away from Steemit, which keeps the value of Steemit.

Ark

Ark is known for their SmartBridge technology. This technology allows people to link different blockchains together through their bridging method. Think about linking together the Lisk blockchain and Ethereum blockchain.

Their team is also pretty competent. Some of them have helped develop Crypti and Lisk. They also have other amazing features like an interplanetary file system, physical card system, optional privacy, and fast transaction speed. It's a coin that looks to be on the rise.

Siacoin

Currently ranked in the top 40 of cryptocurrencies, Siacoin has a market cap of just higher than $200 million. 28 billion Siacoins are in circulation, and it will quickly reach its cap of over 40 billion.

The value of this coin comes from the fact that it is one of the few coins that have a product. It has a decentralized storage space that has better safeguards from hackers when compared to the other mainstream cloud services. It will likely be able to compete with cloud storages provided by Google Drive, Microsoft Dropbox, and Amazon S3, at a lower price. The price for their service will be affected by the market forces.

Paying less for cloud storage is what Siacoin hopes to achieve. You need 2,000 Siacoins to be able to use this service. You will also get the chance to rent out space to others. Since the coins and storage are limited, the value will definitely increase.

It does have some competition with Storj and Maid Safe coin.

Monero

Monero has better anonymity than Bitcoin, which is the reason why its worth was able to go up from $50 to $125 in only a few days. The biggest reason to keep Monero is the user anonymity. There are a lot of sophisticated and intricate methods to create this privacy. It can be broken down into several different methods.

It makes use of a stealth address. If you trade with other types of coins, you will probably see a destination address, and this means that others are able to track you. Monero only displays cryptographic hashes for the destination address. The recipient and sender are the only two people who can read the hash.

They make use of separate transaction units. Let's say you send 100 XMR; it will be delivered to the recipient in separate sums of 30, 20, and 50 XMR. They are each recoded separately, making it harder to track. They also use ring signatures to mix up the transactions and to make anonymity possible.

Ethereum

Ethereum is seen as the best alternative to Bitcoin, and you can see this in its price. In September 2017 it traded at $380. The biggest success for Ethereum is its introduction of the Ethereum network. It made programming on blockchain a lot easier, and this is the reason why there are so many popular coins that are based on this network. Golem and OmiseGo are two great options.

Smart contracts are another reason why Ethereum is so popular. Bitcoin's smart contract consists of sending and receiving coins. Ethereum's smart contracts take things to a whole new level. It gives people the change to manage agreements and makes sure that a payment is made when it is supposed to be.

OmiseGo

This coin is based in Thailand and provides Southeast Asia Stripe-like payment features. The coin is based on Ethereum's network, and it provides the user with real-time payment services and value exchange across jurisdictions. It also lets a user exchange both cryptocurrencies and fiat currencies.

Holders of OMG will be able to make money through transaction fees. The more transactions there are, the more money a holder will make. Because of this, the price of OMG will rise.

The best part of OMG is their financial transaction, which includes business to business commerce, payments, loyalty programs, remittances, and more. They are also done in an inexpensive way.

Iota

As of right now, Iota is the only coin that isn't based on blockchain. It has a new data transfer and transactional settlement layer for the internet of things. The coin is based on a distributed ledger known as Tangle, and its goal is to overcome the problems of blockchain.

Theoretically, it has no transaction fees, unlimited transaction rate, and no miners. This means that it does not have a scalability problem. It also gives people the chance to use small nanopayments. You are also unable to split a coin.

So What Should You Do?

With digital currencies, nobody can be for certain. There is always a risk when getting involved in cryptocurrencies, especially if you choose to invest in them. There is a chance that a $50 coin could end up being worth 50 cents the next day. The listed coins above have a good chance of continuing to rise in value, which means it is a good idea to hold them. As far as selling them for a fiat currency, that comes down to you. Keep an eye on the market to see how things are looking for the coin, and then decide whether you would be better off keeping it or selling it.

FUTURE OF CRYPTOCURRENCY

Cryptocurrencies were able to make the jump from an academic concept to reality when Bitcoin was launched in 2009. Bitcoin continued to attract more followers in the subsequent years, and in 2013 in caught the attention of the media and investors when it hit a record of $266 per Bitcoin. Bitcoin has carried a market value of more than two billion dollars at its peak, but then it experienced a 50% plunge, which caused a raging debate about the cryptocurrencies future. Are these currencies going to supplant conventional currencies and become as universal as the euro and dollar? Or are they more of a passing fad that will fade away in a few years? Bitcoin seems to hold the answer.

The Current Standard

The decentralized nature of Bitcoin makes it free from interference or manipulation of the government. It also means that there isn't a central authority to make sure that everything runs smoothly or anything to back its value. The digital coins are created through mining that requires computers to figure out complex algorithms. The current rate of creation is 25 Bitcoins every ten minutes, and the amount is capped at 21 million, which is expected to be reached in the year 2140.

This is what makes Bitcoin so different from the regular fiat currencies, which has the backing of its government. Fiat currencies are centralized and supervised by a central bank of a nation. While a bank is in control of how much of the currency is given in accordance with the policy, there isn't an upper limit to how much can be issued. Deposits are typically insured against any failures of the bank by a governing body. Bitcoin does not have any of these support mechanisms. Bitcoin's value is completely dependent on what investors will pay for it at any given time. If a Bitcoin exchange were to fold up, the people who have Bitcoin balances have no way of getting them back.

The transaction anonymity and decentralization benefits of Bitcoin have also made it a favorite payment for a lot of illegal activity, which include weapons procurement, smuggling, drug peddling, and money laundering. This has caused it to attract the attention of government agencies like the SEC, Financial Crimes Enforcement Network, Department of Homeland Security, and FBI. The FinCEN issued new rules in March 2013 that defined these virtual administrators and exchanges as money service businesses, which brought them within the scope of government regulation. In May of the same year, the DHS froze a Mt. Gox account that was held at Wells Fargo, saying that anti-money laundering laws were broke. Then on August, 22 emerging payment companies were issued subpoenas by New York's Department of Financial Services. Many of these companies handled Bitcoin. The subpoenas looked to find out the measures they were taking to prevent money laundering, and how they would ensure consumer protection.

Bitcoin Alternatives

Despite the issues it has had, Bitcoin's growing visibility and success has caused several companies to unveil alternative coins, like:

- Litecoin – presently, this altcoin is seen as Bitcoin's biggest rival. It was created to process small transactions faster. Unlike the computer horsepower you need for Bitcoin, Litecoin can be mined using a normal computer. Litecoin has a max of 84 million coins, which is four times more than Bitcoin's limit.

- Ripple – OpenCoin launched Ripple. The payment mechanism for Ripple allows for funds transfers in any currency to a Ripple use in a matter of seconds, which is a big difference to Bitcoin's ten-minute confirmation.

- MintChip – Unlike most other altcoins, MintChip was created by a government institution. This currency is a smart card that has an electronic value, and it can be transferred between chips. MintChip does not require any personal identification, but it is backed by the Canadian dollar.

The Future

The current limitations that cryptocurrencies face, like a person's digital fortune being erased by a crash, or a virtual vault being ransacked by a hacker, could be overcome in time with new advances. What's harder to fix is the paradox of cryptocurrencies: the more they grow in popularity, the more government regulation and scrutiny that will attract, which will eventually erode the fundamental purpose.

While there may be a growing number of merchants who accept these cryptocurrencies, they are still a minority. For them to become used more widely, they will need to gain widespread acceptance among their users. Their complexity, when compared to other currencies, will probably deter people, except for those that are technically adept.

A cryptocurrency that is looking to become part of the mainstream financial world will have to satisfy a wide array of criteria. It will need to be mathematically complex to fight off hackers, but easy enough for the regular consumer to understand. It should be decentralized, but have enough safeguards for consumer protection. It also needs to keep user anonymity without it being used for money laundering, tax evasion, and other illegal activities.

Since all of this is a lot to satisfy, there is a chance that some of the popular cryptocurrencies out there, in a few years, could develop attributes that lie between today's cryptocurrencies and regulated fiat currencies. While this seems like a remote possibility, there is very little doubt that Bitcoin's success in handling these challenges may determine the outlook for altcoins in the coming years.

CONCLUSION

Thanks for making it through to the end of *Cryptocurrency Mining*. Let's hope it was informative and able to provide you with all of the tools you need to achieve your goals.

The next step is to use the information you have learned to help you start your mining rig. Mining cryptocurrencies can be very rewarding if you do things the right way. Continue to research more, and become an amazing miner.

Finally, if you found this book useful in any way, a review on Amazon is always appreciated!

www.ingramcontent.com/pod-product-compliance
Lightning Source LLC
Chambersburg PA
CBHW070201230526
45471CB00002B/757